ABOUT THE AUTHOR

Sharena Lee Satti is an independent spoken word artist and poet from Bradford, West Yorkshire.

She is a very passionate about her work and writes poetry about her own personal life, current environmental issues, social stigmas, homelessness, poverty and discrimination. She speaks openly about her past and the struggles she had to endure. She found her voice and encourages others to find theirs through poetry and self-expression.

She shares her love of spoken word through performance art. She is an influential, uplifting voice in Bradford, spreading her empathy and love of poetry in her local community. Sharena has been nominated for the British Indian Awards, Media Arts and Culture and has recently been associated with Chelping, Red Bull Amaphiko, Film and Photographer Tim Smith and Balbir Dance, Kala Sangam (The Artist Takeover) Bradford Festival, Bradford Literature Festival, The NHS, The South Square Arts Centre, Mend, Bradford Producing Hub, Saltaire Festival, Ilkley Lit Festival, Bradford Libraries, Leeds Lieder, BBC Leeds, Drystone Radio, BCB Radio, BBC Radio 4.

She has facilitated spoken word events and has worked closely with schools delivering poetry workshops.

Instagram: @sharenaleesatti
Twitter: @SharenaLSatti

Sharena Lee Satti

She - (new and selected poems)

VERVE
POETRY PRESS
BIRMINGHAM

PUBLISHED BY VERVE POETRY PRESS
https://vervepoetrypress.com
mail@vervepoetrypress.com

FIRST PUBLISHED NOV 2020
REPRINTED JAN 2021

Printed and bound in the UK
by ImprintDigital, Exeter

ISBN: 978-1-912565-47-4

SHE is dedicated to everyone - the young the old, the lost the broken, the living but unheard. This book exists because what is broken can be repaired. The voiceless can be heard and unhealthy cycles in life can be healed.

CONTENTS

Thankyous

She

from
Testing Times

My Darkened Veil

It's a veil I keep up, it's my shield and it's my protection
My camouflaged armor that keeps me safe from rejection
I hide away and there's a reason why I stay at the back of a queue
I have suffered with anxiety in the past and it's just something I do
To stay un-noticed from your sight as I feel safe hidden from your
thoughts and vision
I've always felt more comfortable this way, been anyone's last choice
or decision
You may see me and think, gosh she's so stuck up, and that's just me
being shy
I'm the type of person to keep my head down so no-one can say hi
It's easier to do that than to be liked and to be known
Me, my thoughts and being alone
I sometimes don't know what to say when I'm writing something in
response to a conversation
The words just won't flow, I'm no good at making communication
I over think and over think, it goes around ten times and I still go
back to saying the same
But you know what, I'm not to blame
I know this now and I'm learning to try & let go of my darkened veil
Yes, I'm an adult, but I'm still a sensitive soul and my emotions are
frail
Every day, as a new challenge arises and I'm trying to push this little
voice from within.
To speak out loud, to run with the wind, to star jump in a crowded
place, to scream, to sing
I'm trying to build my own confidence with every step I take
So forgive me if I say *thankyou* a hundred times or sound like a fruit
cake
It's just when you say good things to me, it's so hard to believe it's
real.

I don't know how to respond to compliments, it's just how I feel
Sometimes my words just don't seem enough
It's just this self-doubt has been with me since a child and yes, it's been quite tough
Despite that I choose to keep taking these little steps of pure light
Knowing one day, I will have full vision and the darkened veil will be out of my sight.

Anxiety

Heart rate increasing with every breath that's drawn deep into the lungs
Words refusing to leave the mouth, shivering in fear stopping on their tongues
Sweat dripping underneath every garment of clothing worn
All eyes on them as if they're a bloody unicorn
Hands in the mouth, it's kind of a distraction
Biting down on all the nails piercing the skin to avoid interaction
Hair down or partially covering the face, a normal disguise
To protect them from all prying eyes
Telling themselves this will soon pass, just breathe in the air and stay strong?
Anxiety can strike at any time, there is no right time or wrong
It sometimes attacks at a time of uncertainty or just on a normal sunny day
Releasing a dense fog blinding your vision, so you can't see your way
It prevents you from living like the normal folks and fear becomes your friend
Due to the deep emotions you feel you can't fully comprehend
The anxious thoughts going around in your mind
Creating its own demons you feared you wouldn't find
It stops you from living as a normal member of society
Trapped in another dimension called anxiety.

from
Broken Chains

Being A Woman

As a foetus we all lay cushioned inside our mother's womb, listening to the endless echoes of her voice
Until one day we are pulled down by gravity's force. The Pain strikes her leaving her gasping to breathe, yet she has no choice
For this child will be born, through each dagger that strikes her, ripping at her uterus as the mother screams out. Consumed by her fears and complete self-doubt
It is through a woman that our lives were created, every blood cell gathered, her body perfected us and protected us from every mortal thing
Yet man, the same human being women gives birth too, can drag her through the streets, with a fist in her face, like a rag doll in a boxing ring
I know not all men are the same but there are still the twisted few, who feel they have the right to abuse women like me and you
You can't even walk down the streets today, with a little lipstick on, without a beep from a car or whit whoo
Expecting some sort of reply, slurring abuse because you ignore and walk by
How dare we be judged by the garments of clothing and the shoes that we wear!
How the hell is this still happening to us. Not able to walk down the street at night, how is this fair?
Women are the healers and the soul receivers of this earth, we plant the seeds and watch life as it's reborn
Men think they can pull us off the street because ripping at our clothes fulfils their needs better than porn
No way shall we fall to the evil and wrongs of man, for us women are here to stand for our freedom and for our very right
That no man shall stop us in the wake of this fight, for we are women and we will walk free in the night

As a foetus we all lay cushioned inside our mother's womb, listening
Free from your insults and free from your cryptic vision, for man
exists because of me, because of you, because of every woman on
this earth
A woman's body is her body to dress it as she pleases, her breasts
are the very breasts that fed you at birth
Her body was the house that shielded and protected every limb of
your body, for woman should be free of your judgement, free of
your curse
Our body is not a toy for no man to play or destroy. A woman is
more than the flesh that you see
Her beating heart is the core of the earth and her soul is the light
that sparkles in every ripple of the sea
So I take stand with and for my sisters that no man will cage me, for
we are women of this earth and we shall walk free.

Destiny Or Fate

Every letter that's spilled across the pages I write
Comes with a little bit of me and the struggles I've had to fight
I have a vision of my future self and where I want to be
The only person that can take me there is this little voice inside
of me
For a long time I've hidden in the shadows just to avoid mankind
Too scared of what was out there or what I would find
Until the day I was blessed with fruits that I had planted
I knew for the sake of their lives I had to pursue this gift I had been
granted
I wanted to give them a childhood that I only had a glimpse of
when I closed my eyes
A happy home filled with laughter and love not heartache and cries
I needed to release the emotions inside so my spirit could be set
free
Writing was my therapy, it allowed me to grow and become who I
wanted to be
Nothing has come easy but each struggle is a blessing in disguise
At the time I cursed life but I put my trust in God, for he is the
all-knowing and the all-wise
I don't like to plan my future, I just flow with the waves and swim
against the tide
For you never know what tomorrow will bring and who will be by
your side
Life can sometimes take you off course and your path seems
unclear
You get lost in the midst of its fog and possessed by its fear
Yet in its absence it reveals a new path you missed before
Revealing a new spring adventure ready for you to explore.

Sirius

Lost in the deep layers of darkness, my eyes fixated on you
Do you notice me, as I notice you? From such heights, featuring the
world view?
Your oracle has frozen my vision, never to thaw out, paralyzed
For I seek no escape, it is I who is truly hypnotized
I see only you, a light reflecting in the dark
Who ignites the flame and passion, but why the big question mark?
I wonder what lurks in your endless skies that have forbidden me
to love
Anyone else but you, watching down on me from up above
I seek your knowledge and strength, your guidance and willpower
Such force generated, that tames this wild flower
For I am captivated by your presence, I want to get closer, I need to
see
Why does staring at you set my spirit free?
I could sit for hours in the darkness, only to follow your light, in the
distance
For you give me hope of a new existence
I lose myself in your honor, you replenish my soul and awaken my
senses
Cleansing my spirit and freeing me from all worldly pretences
I want to levitate to your world beyond the clouds, touching the
passing sky
Shed free from the chrysalis, reborn a butterfly
Possessed by your power, it's truly bizarre
Captivated by your presence,
SIRIUS the night STAR.

from
Unapologetic

Mental Health

Mental health has no age restrictions, it has no laws
It enters all homes, digging deep, with its claws
It can lay dormant, silently still
Until one day when you lose your will
Your will to move, to breathe, to look and believe
That you can make it through
Or to take a step back and see value in your life
Mental health can creep up on us at any time
Even in your highest glory when you feel alive
It can send you crashing down in an ocean,
Drowning in a sky dive
Mental health attacks every thought in one's mind
Leaving its emptiness, its loneliness, its feelings so unkind
Yet no one should feel alone or suffer in silence
At the hands of this mental health violence
Let's banish the stigma and raise our voices, speak up, speak out
Scream that pain and release that self-doubt
Because somebody out there is ready to listen
To hold your hand and listen
To help bring back that sparkle inside you're missing
Recovery takes time, we need to heal the mind
You cannot see mental health, even if our eyes are not blind
One needs to take the first step to acknowledge what they're feeling
And no, you are strong enough, to start this healing
Let's start to rebuild, brick by brick, stone by stone
Recovery is a process and you are not alone
Let's dance in the sun rays of hope and
Find healing ways that help u cope
With your Mental health, we can do this.

She Is A Warrior

A flame of fire, a piece of art
Everyone desired a piece of her heart
She was a wanted woman, she wanted no man
She was rebellious and never stuck to no plan
A real change maker, tough as iron steel
Even if she didn't allow her pain to heal
She was fierce, and would never back down
To anyone who tried to knock off her crown
She was chaotic in her own beautiful way
Her face was something that should have been on display
Beauty that concealed her soul from her painful past
Born unwanted and seen as the outcast
Yet she never let it show
She planted her pain and watched her flower grow
Heather she grew amongst fields, not swamped in the mildew
Painting landscapes and highlands, a lavender view
She radiated power, electrical waves
She was the world's strength, she was the brave
She took on the world and stood alone
In a world she was never accepted on her own
A fighter, a warrior, slaying her demons on the battle field
With her bare hands and no shield
She is my warrior, her strength is now mine
As the wind blows, passing down our blood line
I will always remember her wars and battle scars
As she aligned the hearts of moons and stars
Only the brave as she fought on,
Decades later and still holding on
Praying for my own strength to keep me strong
For her one day.

He Is Sorry

He rips apart her soul with the venom he spills from his tongue
She can't breathe, he has clenched his fist around her lung
Piercing holes with the pressure, blood descending from the eyes
Frazzling her brain with his vicious lies and then he goes on to apologise
Along as he's sorry, in his mind its ok, everything has gone away
He said *sorry*. He has cleansed his pallet, now welcome dessert
He's happy right, all forgotten as he starts to unbutton his blue checked shirt
He forgets so easily, as she sits there with his words spinning in a cyclone, powerless to move
Her body jolting with each thrust, showing his force, the power he must prove
He said *sorry* right, he loves her too
Yes every time he jumps up and down on her heart ripping the blood from her skin tissue
He is sorry? When he brakes her down piece by piece, slowly decaying, under his spell
Eating away at her energy, drawing the light to his hell
He is sorry, right?
So sorry that he will continue to burn your thoughts at the stake
Sending tremors through the waves, obliterated by his earthquake
Pouring his own selfish affliction all over you
Binded by your lack of value, you just don't see
How fucked up he is mentally
Using you, confusing you, abusing you
But he loves you right?

I Didn't Think I'd See This Day

As a child I'd wish my life away
Even held hands with the angel of death
Yet he refused to take my last breath
I begged him several times or more, to let me leave
Let me die in peace, yet he held this belief
That one day this life would be something I'd be speaking up for
Not ever in my wildest dreams, even through my crazy teens
Did I believe my life could be restored
I sipped poison slowly every day
Drinking my daily medicine, that made me feel ok
It blocked out the pain, made me feel human again
It was the norm to smoke weed in your time of need
and forget it all, I didn't think I'd see this day
When I wouldn't be intoxicated by alcohol
And a cigarette burning in the ashtray
Sat with all the other lost kids, wishing our life away
I didn't see my future path, frozen in a time
Where life was a blur and streets where filled with crime
Yet I held this dream one day I'd break free
Of this side of me, and that I didn't have to be
A lost child anymore, a child of no one, maybe by name or down
on paper
Absent parental responsibilities, burning its own toxic vapour
I tried my best to see the good in me and what could potentially be
My future, what if I broke free and released this caged me
How different life would be
This warrior inside of me wouldn't allow this pain to breed
To feed, no way was this darkness going to succeed
I held onto hope and I kept on going, I kept on believing
That one day I'd break free and see this future day.

Finding My Voice

I once held onto the silence,
The dead mute, the empty darkness
As my eyes screamed to be heard
I stood still, didn't speak a single word
I released a fragile smile
My thoughts were producing fruits, my mind so fertile
I silently craved to be heard
To release my voice from within
That was prying the blood from my skin
Yet I stayed silent, too afraid to speak
Seen as vulnerable and weak
I have this beast inside I need to unleash
Hidden in the prison I created, afraid to release
Yet this voice needs to be free
It's seeping through the pours in my skin
I need to release it from within
Yet I'm not sure if I'm ready or if others are ready to see
Me as strong and unique, not vulnerable and weak
As I breathe out deeply
I have to release this voice that's suppressing me
Alongside the beast that's held in my captivity
It's the only way to release my voice
But releasing one will set them both free
The devil will rejoice but at least my voice will be free.

21st Century Women

I want to see Women empowering women, sisters of all nations
joining together
Like Daisies creating links of life, defying the change in the weather
Blossoming next to each other, supporting each sister, nourishing
each other's growth
Connecting roots together, bonding through silence, not oath
I want to see women comfortable in their own skin
Sharing who they truly are, the beauty deep within
Women standing fiercely together producing heat that no water can
tame
Women united as one spreading like wildfire, ignited by just one
flame
I want to see powerful women in the media spreading real news
Highlighting the real issues. Like me-too and all the damn right
abuse
The women shown in our magazines, on TV, have a duty to our
youth
To highlight the wrongs in the industry and stop covering up the
truth
Models starving to fit into society's dream, while school girls follow
Skipping their meals at dinner or just bringing the food to their lips,
but it's a crime to swallow
It's the Women in communities who really strive for change, who
give the isolated women a voice
Opening up doors of opportunity and windows of choice
It's arts and creative spaces that are bringing communities together,
creating hope
Women networking together, jumping of cliffs, not fearful of who is
holding their rope
No bitchiness, no jealousy, just women helping women, fighting for
each other

Speaking out against the wrongs of the world, thinking of children in Palestine or helping the single mother.
I want to see a world where women work together like the ladies in the communities
Who dedicate their time to open a world of opportunities
It's these women who should have their own TV show, be in every newspaper, sharing their views
The real women, helping real people, not fabricating the news
We are the fruits of the soil, the women of this earth
The healers and the soul receivers, granting life as we give birth
No longer stuck in old traditions, we are the change, we hold the power
To continue rewriting history and help the growth of every flower
We stand together as one, we are the change the suffragettes wanted us to see
So we stand here proudly together, in their honour, recreating History.

I Am

I am the rescued, the eerie silence left, the awkward pause, I am the
visible light
I am the question mark, the lost but not the missing, I am the girl
with the stage fright
I am the living, the breathing, the let's get all excited, daffodils are
appearing, kind of girl
I am a mixture of seasons, rain droplets falling, over sunny
rainbows, as warm winds swirl
I am the darkness that penetrates deep beyond the layers of skin
that conceal my soul
The fog that blurs the sadness, the crazy mess, the madness, the loss
beyond my control
I am the fragile, not the weak, the over thinking, the overeating the
self-body hate
I am the antisocial, the trying communicator who would prefer to
hibernate
I am the clear skies on a summer's day for everybody else except me
I am the smile, not always the happy image you see, who is not
afraid to unmask her vulnerability
I am the passing storm, the wild, the wonderful, the free
I am the dandelion growing amongst the weeds, I am the salt in the
sea
I am the little voice calling, the lioness roaring, I am me
I am not the first word that enters your thoughts, I am more
More than the words I harvest, more than the words I speak up for
I am the wind, dancing amongst the rain droplets that form
puddles in the street
I am the star-gazer, the moon lover, the incomplete
I am work in progress, completing the puzzle piece by piece
What you see on the surface is not always what is happening
underneath.

I am a whirlwind of emotions, I have fought my own demons on the battle ground
I'm my own worst enemy at times but I'm no push around
I am the girl who gets lost in the heavenly skies and is infatuated with butterflies
I am more than I even see, for beauty lies in the sunrise and I need to start loving me.

Two Fingers To You

Not everyone will like what you do
Neither will they be happy for you
When you spread your wings and start to shine
The grapes turn sour in their once pleasing wine
You become the venom spilled from their tongue
The more you blossom, the more jealous they become
Masked and suited, you'd never guess
These lost spirits who slander, their lives a mess
Using their dark energy to burn through the soul
Like it grants them access to the window of control
You feel their presence, the burn, the heat
The negative energy, the lies and deceit
You feel this, you don't see this, its masked cleverly
Two fingers up to your negative energy.

Dying To Be Thin

She smiles, showering a rainbow of light
Yet deep inside is a hidden pain that she is struggling to fight
The demons that haunt her, that taunt, that call her name
You see her everlasting smile that disguises her shame
She is lost in the figures that run daily through her mind
Controlled by the mirror, the all-seeing non blind
It's that very image that destroys her each and every day
Cloaking her hell under Heaven's light, a burning display
She is cursed by a vision she sees daily, it clings to her flesh
Wishing she could contain the evil inside a titanium mesh
Squeeze it all inside, squeeze the tissues to fit in
Suffocate the growth and make her feel thin
Addicted to the sweet taste that drips from her lips, that makes
her feel whole
Swirling the chocolate as it soaks into her saliva, intoxicating
her soul
Frozen in that very moment, silent, till bang-lightening comes
crashing down
And in the rain she begins to drown
The guilt rips at her thoughts, she is sinking, drowning in her
own tears
Controlled by her eating disorder that awakens her fears
It's a cycle, an addiction that she cannot escape
Unless she stops eating food altogether to keep in shape
The struggle is real hidden behind her smile.

I Said No

What part of *no* did u not understand
When you grabbed my hand
And you refused to let go
When I screamed *No*
And you didn't let go
When you pushed me to the floor
You whispered I'm your whore
Like that should give me some comfort
As you ripped at my clothes
And started to expose
My naked flesh, my skin
Pushing your body on mine, penetrating in
What part of *no* did you not understand
When you prised open my legs and thrusted your hand
Into me
When you licked the tears off my face
And said this is my pussy
Like you had the permission to touch my body
Could you not hear my screams, my pleas
Of *please leave me?*
Oh yes, you could see
You enjoyed the power and u enjoyed abusing me
Leaving this broken memory, this wreckage left
What you stole from me, wasn't just theft
You ripped apart my very soul
When I said *No*, yet you still had control
OF MY BODY.

Beauty

Fighting a constant battle with myself
To the point that I question its effects on my health
Why am I so uncomfortable in my own skin?
Like my body is mutating within
Why does the word *beautiful* and *I*
Always seem to signify
Something so strikingly painful to me
Like subconsciously, I hate myself
Is it something of the mind?
That doesn't want me to find
My inner beauty
Why do I always believe
I am not meant to receive
Positive words, like *you're pretty*?
How can you define beauty?
When you cannot see
Your soul
Everyone so powered up by their hormones
They lack visibility
Of what being beautiful is truly meant to be
I sometimes look in the mirror
And fail to recognise
The person staring back at me
And I curse that word *beauty*
Stamped by your labels
That enables me to
Be seen as WORTHY.

Finding Faith

I was always a child who held onto her faith
In this world that was once a strange place
Lacking identity and understanding my race
Yet I held on strongly to my faith
In the times I didn't think I'd make it through
And I thought my life was of no value
You see, I grew up on a council estate
Where love wasn't practiced as much as hate
And if you weren't mixed race then no one could relate
I was a lost little child, I was misunderstood
I never believed that I could
Be loved or seen as any good
Until one day I found my way
When I recited my *shahada* and I practiced how to pray
I found a light that began to ignite
When I declared my faith that day
Becoming a Muslim granted me inner peace
It was an instant release
Like breathing in fresh air
I no longer felt alone or confused
My heart was full of gratitude
For my creator who had helped me see
That the path I was on wasn't meant for me
That I wasn't a nobody
And it was my destiny
To be a Muslim.

I Write

I'm not here to please or do a damn strip tease
I write to release the pain
Be the emerging rainbow after the downpour of rain
I write to see a better day
Allowing my thoughts to carry me to a place far away
My ink fills the paper and the paper stares back at me
A running river of emotions, freeing my sanity
I write because my heart burns with an endless desire
A slave to myself that fuels this wild fire
Tamed only by spilling ink onto paper
Releasing emotions that vanish like vapour
Sometimes I feel like I'm suffocating, I'm dying
When my world is crumbling, yet I smile and keep trying
I write because it's inside of me, it's my oxygen, it allows me to
breathe
It's my source of strength that makes me stay when I want to run
and leave
How can I run from myself because of my messed up mental
health?
I just need to breathe
I write better than I speak, I am my own worst critique when the
darkness creeps in
So I write and keep writing till I feel good from within
No longer clouded by darkness or having to endure
For poetry is my one and only cure.

Damaged Goods

They call them damaged goods, kids in care
Kids that live on council estates with parents stuck on child welfare
The forgotten children that authorities want to ignore
Damaged goods, best to lock them away than to let them explore
The kids that commit crime, to get by not do time
Victims of poverty and expectations, these kids cannot climb
One rule for all, kids have to comply to the standards the government set
Go to school and get a degree but they fail to tell you, you will be riddled with debt
They call them damaged goods but they never give the kids a chance to grow
Living in care or wrapped in the council estate bubble is all they know
Some kids are left to fend for themselves
Forgotten about like dusty books sitting on shelves
Who is there to push these kids' dreams and allow them to breathe
To show these kids how to break free from this negativity and help them achieve
Their dreams their desires and show them how to believe
In themselves when they have no one and they're alone
Stuck in the destruction of a spinning cyclone its wreckage left, that they call home?
A home life is never a good life, it's surviving and making it through
Damaged goods they say, like we are the disease of one's DNA that riddles in your skin tissue
When you live in an estate you're locked at the gate, through the bars they let you peep through
To a world you have never seen and dreams so distant that you can barely view

These kids are not damaged goods just misunderstood
Trying to live life and survive and make it through their childhood
Damaged goods is the systems way to say we won't survive
That we will end up on drugs or locked up because we're thugs
But I am proof we can make it out alive.

New
poems

A Recipe To Understanding Her

You need an open heart, as open as the universe
Your love needs to be resilient like the darkness of a curse
You need a few drops of sweetener
For when she's feeling bitter
Or she will frazzle your brain like a 5G transmitter
Usually around the full moon or her pmt
She needs a few days of silence where she can be
Her own tidal wave or crashing sea
You will need a course in crash landing
When you feel she is becoming too demanding
It's a trigger, she's silently seeking your attention
Something she has not yet mentioned,
Because she's feeling a little raw
A little insecure and she needs a spoonful of your warmth
On her forehead, your soft lips just resting there
In that silence she knows you care
She needs a life time of truth, not even a droplet of a lie
Always best to reply with the truth
You need to smile more, make her laugh daily
Joke and be silly, act a little crazy
Look in her eyes whenever she looks in yours
Just pause, for a few seconds, embrace this moment
Leave the window to the soul open
Like an ocean, let it pool over your soul
Take control of that ego
And know when you let love flow
You leave that window open, to understand her better
She's the one your heart chose
Treasure that you met her.

Broken Branch

I am the broken branch that falls alone
Leaving life as I knew it, to enter the unknown
Not protected by the roots that once enriched my soul
To the beholder, that didn't see the power or control
I am the broken branch that's fallen with dying leaves
Still clinging to life, rustling in the breeze
Drinking from the soil and the open clouds
An outcast amongst the trees
Trying to survive the loneliness, the whispers in the night
From the decaying poison that breeds after daylight
I am the broken branch that still has the will
To live, to grow from the nothing that I have become
Scattered broken pieces and a restless heart so numb
For I am the nothing, you said I'd become
With roots that blossom when I breathe
And leaves that grieve when they fall
I am everything and all you said I wouldn't be
I stand, re planted in the dirt you throw at me
Tiny petals forming on the stem of my body
I am not the broken branch that fell to the floor
Or your empty words of nothing, I am more
More than you could ever possibly see
Because when you look at me
You only see things visually
Always using your one angle perspective
To show how affective your power can be
Leaving a broken branch
You thought you had destroyed me
Yet for me to be free I had to fall.

A Connection

An invisible wave, a flowing energy
A light inside that's penetrating me
It's the comfort of your silence in a place
That I no longer feel alone, a space
Carved with your imprints
Imbedded into my thoughts
That you fully support me
It's the cloudy haze
I feel when you steal my soul
Blinded by my emotions, I lose control
Of me, I cannot see
Clearly, all I see is a blank space
A midnight sky, a super full moon
Illuminated by flickers of light
You spark up this appetite
Leaving this hunger, this deep longing to be
Youy crashing wave, your echo in the sea
I want to be, your colour changing sky
When night falls, the red sky swirls into blue
And the last of the light shines through
I want to be stood right beside you
It's our connection, our invisible emptiness of
Craziness, of fantasy and fiction
You are my addiction, my galaxy away from earth
You are the key to my rebirth
The light inside of me
It's our connection, this invisible energy
Linking these roots that are pulling me
To you.

Only Today

Who says tomorrow is promised?
Not a soul if I'm honest, life is never promised
Most live to buy a house, a car or fund a degree
Set a date for a wedding and start a family
It's how we are programmed to be
To live our life systematically
What if today was our last and the ending was never forecast
Can you truly say you have embraced each and every day?
Will your good deeds outweigh your wealth?
Do you ever spend a moment just thinking of yourself
Filling your body with self-love and good health?
Do you ever look around and appreciate the ground you stand upon?
No, not many do, until it's too late and then you're gone
To appreciate the real things that matter, that count
Helping others, not concerned about your bank account
Don't be one of those that are fuelled by greed
Who always feel the need to live up to society's expectations
Changing the very foundations they once believed
What if we only had today?
Would you remember God, would you pray?
How would you spend your last living day?
What are the things you regret, the things you didn't do?
What held you back, what stopped you?
Would you breathe in your last drops of air
Regretting the time you gave to those who pretended to care?
What would you do?
I would pour my heart out too
Myself, my thoughts would consume my body
They would destroy my soul, my lack of power and no control
Of death, I would fear my sins and my lack of good deeds

I would beg for more time to plant more seeds
As my heart bleeds, as my soul cries
Longing to see just one more sunrise
I would regret the times I lived unhappy
To suit others why could I never hear my own plea?
Why did I always choose to ignore me?
What if you looked into the future and saw this day?
Would you return to your old life, would you change your way?
What would you learn?
Value life for to the earth we shall return.

Thankyou

Thank you for fuelling my ammunition tank
With your systematic critique
I don't write to please others
It's my own technique
I write for me
To release this inner energy
That's brewing inside of me
That's reaching to the light
That's craving to be free
Thank you for showing me
That I am special
That I can hold my tongue
When I haven't even begun
To express how I feel
When I didn't reveal
How much I truly hate
People who demotivate others
What is the need to knock others down
Who want to succeed
At picking themselves off the ground?
Thank you for showing me
The person I never want to be
With your judgemental inspections
I'll never strive for perfection
And that's ok with me
You will not supress my creativity
For I am living and breathing
Because of writing my poetry.

To Live Free

We are the endless sky, the invisible air, the open sea
We are the footprints in the sand
We are the land that connects roots to tree
We are the explorers of rubble and broken stone
We are the voices that scream for peace in a war zone
We are the silent whispers that decrease
Alongside each bullet unleashed
We are the eyes that crave to see more than blood and bone
We are the withered memories of yesterday's dream
We are the smiles of what could have been
Had our lands not seen war
Yet no-one is held accountable for
The genocide, the ethnic cleansing, that's caused by war
We are the broken memories, the scattered pieces
We are the voices that rejoice in the street when life is born
We have seen more death than our bodies can mourn
Now do you understand, why we want to reach safe land?
Do you understand that peace always comes at a price?
Under your rules and politics,
We will always be an easy sacrifice
Now tell me who cares about my life
When will one start to begin
To see my life as more than layers of flesh and skin
To see my life as having some worth
A human being that belongs on this earth
Not just a migrant or a refugee?
When will people understand I just want to live free?
Live without fear of death, or people hunting my family
To breathe in clean fresh air that's not thick with smoke
To sit amongst whole trees, no branches broke

To eat without limitations, be free from starvation
I yearn for peace, to live free
Then I won't have to live in your country.

My Moon

I await your arrival like the bees wait for spring
Released from hibernation to taste life once again
I await your arrival to heal the cracks that cause my suffering
To seal the emptiness from which I'm still recovering
I await your arrival to revive my soul
To synchronise my depleted energy flow
I await your arrival so I can finally feel in control
Of the days when I'm alone and craving your presence
Mourning your nonexistence, waiting for your essence
You left me, you left this soul and handed my heart to a new host
You left me, lifeless, in a world of life, leaving just your ghost
You left me with your memories, my light into the dark
You left me with a light I want to demolish
A light only you could ignite
I'm missing my taste of your heavenly rays
When darkness falls and clouds my days
I'm missing my oxygen, my daily fuel
Where my heart takes a rest and it cannot rule
My thoughts or thinking because I have you
And as much as I love my skies so blue
I know that after twenty nine days have passed
I'll eventually see you, and that doesn't stop me
From missing you like silence misses its secrecy
I want to tune into your frequency
That has me questioning
This invisible wave, this incredible electricity
That haunts me when you're not around
You are the spark in my heart that disappears far too soon
Nothing comes close to you, my dear Moon.

How Do I Tell You?

How do I tell you I'm afraid
Afraid of the very thoughts that linger in my mind
How I wish to be a memory left behind?
How do I tell you I'm tired, I'm tired of trying
To live this life when I feel like I'm dying?
How do I tell you I just want to disappear
Vanish from the earth and be free from fear?
How do I tell you my body feels heavy, dragged down, trapped
Lost within the flesh and bones, my soul kidnapped?
How do I tell you, I see no colour, I see no light
Surrounded by darkness, no future in sight?
How do I tell you, when you won't believe it yourself
It's such a taboo to talk about mental health?
How do I tell you tomorrow I will take my last breath?
I will leave you my smile but hold hands with the angel of death?
How do I tell you?
You tell me
Break free of these thoughts and you tell me
Find the strength to scream out because I cannot live without
You, you tell me, help me see the pain you mask so well
Together we will break free from the chains in your hell
You tell me we can banish the demons in your head
That are playing games, telling you you're better off dead
You tell me, you tell me and know I love you
For your life is my life and we will make it through
You tell me
You tell me.

I Survived

I should have crumbled under the pressure of everyday life
I'm lucky to even be alive, to be standing here
I've dived into the darkest sea and I've drowned in its fear
I was once a child trapped in a whirlwind of domestic violence
and poverty
I was hungry for a life that didn't choose me
I held onto my faith that one day I'd see
A better life, a sweet escape, something for me
To change this damn reality that I'm living every day
Struggling to survive this hard hitting life that's suppressing me
I failed to fit in at school or stick to any rule
Because I had too much going on at home
And my thoughts would continuously roam
Trying to block out the alcoholic fuelled fights
That would happen every other night
Or the ambulance's blue flashing lights
I still believed that this life wasn't meant for me
That I'm more than worthy of my life being happy
Being loved for me, no expectations
No family complications or being seen as a nobody
Always seen as the outcast
The kid that didn't last at school or take any GCSEs
Because whilst the other kids were studying
I was still mothering my younger siblings and my family
I missed out on my education, I fought back the frustration
That was destroying me
I pulled myself together and took on my own responsibility
I knew one thing for sure
I would never endure or suffer anymore
This life that was forced upon me
So I decided to erase that path and write my own destiny.

I Am Needy

I want you all, I need to feel complete
Even missing one grain of sand in the desert's heat
Would make me feel incomplete, if it was touched by your hands
and your delicate feet
I'm needy, my soul feeds from your magnetic vibrations
That pulsing sensation, I need more, more than a feeling
A deeper meaning, a sensual healing
I want to be loved, squeezed, held tight and caressed
I want you to invest your time in me, every second that passes I
want you to be
Here with me, I'm needy and I need you more than your very own
heart beating
More than your lungs breathing, I can't help this feeling
Of needing you more than you can give, even if giving is more
than you can give
I need more of you for me to live
I'm needy, not every day or every week, it just happens now and
again
When I feel at a low and I know I cannot complain
Because I have your full complete attention, yet I'm still needy
So greedy for more, intoxicated by your loving, it leaves me
craving more
I want you to explore this body, you hold the map in your hands
That leads you to safe lands, where you can explore more than this
shore
And dance in my heavenly sea, I need you baby
To take me into your soul, I stand naked, skin to skin
That deeper feeling is you, as you breathe life within me
I am needy, I yearn to be in your presence, your very essence daily
This is just me, all of me and how I wish to be touched in the very
places

Your eyes cannot see, I'm not just needy
I need you to tame this body spiritually
Rescue me, with your lips and tongue
Because you my love are not just someone
And I wish I wasn't so needy.

Oh, Mr Dealer

Oh, Mr Dealer
What is this crap you keep feeding her?
I'm struggling to heal her
Oh dealer, do you know you are destroying my mother cell by cell?
While you sit in your paradise, she sits in her hell
You fill your pockets with her next heroin fix
Whilst counting your bank notes
See, she's dying a slow death whilst making you rich
Every time you make your sales pitch
That this shit is a better batch
And it's a better suited match to her requirements
Not retirement as this is a one way trip to death
And you commit murder every time she takes in a breath
Of that toxin that releases in to her blood stream
Your selfish act to fulfil your own needs is taking this to the extreme
Of my Mother's life, whilst you nurture and love your own
You leave me in this life without my own
Oh, Mr Dealer, you're destroying her life
As I am trying to heal her
As long as you are in her life, she will never live any kind of life
She is barely living but keeps giving you every penny she gets
Until she's riddled in debt, a slave to you
Till all that is left of her is bones and skin tissue
You will keep pursuing her, she's your cash flow
Your embedded embryo that you'll never ever let go
You see, Mr Dealer, you soul stealer
You are taking my mother's life
Bit by bit, piece by piece, the slowing of her heart beats
Too many ruining lives running drugs on the streets
Her blood is on your hands.

Suicide Note

Some say suicide is a cry for help
When you get to the point of breaking
When your soul is physically shaking within your hollow skin
You have the pressure of the word and no one or nothing
Is listening to what's going on in your mind
These thoughts, so unkind, are shattering any positive thinking
When you're drowning, when you're sinking
And no-one or nothing knows what you're truly thinking
Because you sit there with a smile
All the while you're suffocating, your bones are being slowly crushed
Into ashes, into dust, like you never existed
Just another suicide listed, another note left with the words *I can't do me*
I'm dying slowly, I'm exhausted mentally and you all looked at me
Endlessly like I could sprinkle life into freshly rooted seeds
Like a timeless flow of water where no poison can breed
Yet no-one ever saw the implanted seeds that I used to feed, myself
The over worrying of everyday things that was eating at my health
The darkness crept in, it stopped me talking, it shut me out from myself
I wanted to cry, I wanted to scream, I wanted drag my thoughts into the light
I wanted someone, anyone, to tell me I'd be alright
I was a prisoner to fear, too afraid to speak
Didn't want to listen to other people's critiques, branding me weak
I didn't want to die, so I wrote this letter
Then the emotions settled and I knew this would never be my final goodbye
Because I   am stronger than this
I never wanted this, I never asked for my thoughts to multiply

I contemplated death but I didn't want to die
I was more alone than the moon in the sky
With each passing cloud I knew I had to survive
This hard hitting life and make a change for me
So here is the end of my suicide note
I will keep fighting and rewriting my own destiny
I will not allow suicide to be the death of me.

What Is Love?

Its unlimited conversations and pauses of silence
It's a language that speaks through every heartbeat
It's a feeling, a sensual kind of healing
That penetrates the soul that has full control of you
And everything that you do, because when you love
You love without limitations or any navigation
Because love takes its own route
It rides through thunder storms and open seas
Tidal waves and a hurricane's breeze
It's like an open sky on a summer's evening
When the sunset fades into the horizon
And you get that warm, fuzzy feeling
Love is an understanding, it's being patient
It's holding it together at the times you want to fall apart
When the beating of your heart pulses
When it palpitates, when life sometimes invalidates how you feel
Love carries you to a place that allows you to heal
Love is wireless, its eye communication
It's an intuition, a spiritual vibration
It's velvet red roses stemmed with pin-pricked thorns
It's the early morning sun rays as a new day dawns
Love is eternal, its more than physical contact
It's loving her soul more than her body in fact
Love is poetry and she is your muse
Your electrical fuse that ignites your heart
Love is a whirlwind of overactive heartbeats
Where eye contact meets
And you know this is the only place you want to be
Where she makes u feel wanted and loved and she shows you
you are worthy
This is Love.

Body Hair

The fine fuzz, the grains of hair that you have on your face
That sits in a place you wish you could hide
Because society now tells us
Of these new beauty treatments and we have to abide
Fall to the latest craze, micro-blading or razorblade
Or hide in shame if you haven't yet had it threaded
Finely plucked from the skin, pulled from the root it's embedded
In, they tell you it will grow back thinner, it will be invisible from the
skin
You don't have to get paranoid when people are talking
Because they are not looking at the hair around your lips
Or noticing the strands that delicately sit
Near your cheekbones, you're blaming your hormones
Even your elders, it must be their fault, right?
That this extra body hair is visible to every eye in sight
These days girls are shaving more than men
And when it grows back they have to repeat it again
But why not leave it alone, leave it to rest as it should
We have become so embroiled in beauty that we have
misunderstood
That erasing one's hair may temporally make you feel good
But it's another decoy for beauty products to get shelved and stocked
Money in consumers' pockets and most images they use are
photoshopped
Redesigned and re-refined to make you believe
That this technique they use will help you achieve
The results you crave, the no stubble hair with a shave
Yet they fail to tell you it will grow back, it will continue to grow
And leave the skin with a green shadow
You will have the headache of not only
Shaving your legs, your armpits, your lady bits

But your face too, I'd rather make do with my imperfect skin
No following, I have girls watching that I need to keep inspiring
Sharing that beauty goes beyond what we see
And we have to keep spreading body-love and body-positivity
So defo, no shaving for me.

Dear Body

I've hated you since I first noticed my breast begin to form
As my hips started to widen and my arse started to transform
Every line, every curve, you cursed me, I've always hated you body
You gave me a woman's body and I was just a child
You triggered eyes like a light switch, sniggers and smiles
That contributed to me hating you
I've never loved you, or liked you, I've pretended to though, many times
Feeding my mind those lies that I love the way my body curves and isn't just a straight line
How it's formed like waves that bathe in my skin, I've always loved the sea
But I've never been able to love you body, or escape from you, me
I've been suffocating under your layers of skin and I've deeply tried to
Love you more than I've hated you
I've tried, trust me I've tried, but every time I said *I look ok today*
I lied, I hated the way my clothes always show every dam curve
I'm sorry I never give you the love you truly deserve
I've always complained and tried to change the way you are
Leaving myself with these mental scars, these deep embedded cruel taunts
That I allowed to saunter in and out of my thoughts to torment my own self
I've never praised you once or thanked you for my health
For holding my internal organs in place, allowing my heart to beat
At the very times you should have admitted defeat
You never gave in, just kept loving me from within
Kept my heart beating, my lungs breathing, you kept me alive
Dear body thank you for this life, I'm sorry I have always sacrificed

This life within, I'm learning to love you more
Every curve, every imperfect flaw,
I'm trying to heal this body dysmorphia war
Starting from the roots, the inner core of the mind
Changing the thoughts of unkindness with love, Love for me.

She's A Goddess

Of this earth, of this whole universe
She is the wild wind that blows in the breeze
That leaves that summer essence clinging to our memories
She is the herbal remedy that quenches your thirst on a summer's
evening
She is the rays of the sun that reflects on your skin and gives you that
sensual feeling
She nurtures every heart beating
From the Earth she rises, her body naked, unclothed, bearing her
fertile fruits
Born from the elements of life that nourish her roots
Like the wise oak tree she inhales and breathes, embedding her
strength through every branch
That swirls and twists creating waves of the ocean in her dimpled
stretched skin
That delicately sits on her loving hips, her body a painted canvas
Dipped in the sparkles from the midnight sky
You cannot measure the strength of her heart
Of the things she's had to endure, her hidden pain and so much more
Her body is a masterpiece of art, of her resilience, of her strength
Of the very length of every ocean she's had to swim
No matter how tired her body has been
She's kept going, moving every limb
Climbing mountains and crossing deserts, never giving in
Her tattoos and the fine ink printing belong on her skin
Like her eyes that breathe life and her cheeks that dimple in
Like the fine lines that engrave deep under her eyes when she smiles
I see the sunrise, I see the light of heaven descending in her
She's fierce as her lioness roar and as gentle as a rain droplet's whisper
She is nature, and from the earth she devours her beauty

Unfiltered and care free, she has this cosmic energy
This electricity, that flows through her blood stream
Fusing the power that she ignites in every wild flower
She is the Mother of Earth, the soul carrier that gives birth
Granting life to the world, she possesses that power
Her body creates life, her organs shift to make room
As she breathes life into her womb
As her skin stretches and tears into fine, red lines of silk
The skin tissue of her breasts behind to fill with milk
Her body is a vessel that she nurtures and protects
For her implanted seed to grow, leaving her skin outstretched
With extra layers of wobbly skin and a little more jelly clinging to
those hips
After the moon and sun entwined together create her total eclipse
She's left loving her extra jelly bits, the lumps and bumps that cling
to her skin
She's a butterfly emerging from her catalyst, her wings spread side
by side
She doesn't hide behind the mask of todays conflicted society
Nor does she listen to the magazines or media that want to change
her reality
She stands true to herself, embracing her uniqueness, acknowledging
she is enough
For this is her story
Practising her own self-love, smiling more, being kinder to herself
Challenging those moments that really affected her health
She is the petals that dance around the sun in a meadow of gold and
yellow
Her morning hello is the first break of light
Her soft whispers leave the mountains longing to sit with her in the
moonlit night.
For she is beautiful, the beauty you see is real, completely
un-photoshopped
Not a bottle sat on a shelf or a product that's been stocked

She has bad hair days, with a smile always and she rocks that style
For who needs hair to release a smile
She is curvy, she is thin, she is breathtaking
An indestructible feminine, bold and brave and all-giving
She is the memories of your past and the stories of your future
She is the flutters in your stomach and the full belly laughs of
humour
She is unpredictable like the seasons when snow falls in spring
Unapologetic, yet truly genuine
She is the Goddess of life, of the living, of the breathing
A human medicine, the all-healing
Her scars rest upon her skin, her pain blossoming
Into flowers, she's transformed that pain into power
Her clothes are a reflection of her individuality
And she bares her soul through her very eyes
Her body lies in the beauty of every sunrise
For she is a Goddess.

Identity

I was once a child with no identity
My body was riddled with DNA cells that my own body rejected
My body was infected with a disease that showed in the pigment
of my skin
Visually you could see the colour of my skin, but were clueless to
the scars I carry within
My bones were formed from the fragments of earth my soul has
never seen
A land I've never touched or ever been, where it smells of sweet
jasmine
And loud people talking in a language that I never understood
Yet that language is connected to me like land meets sea
I am the split of continents, I am your flags combined,
My bloodline is scattered across foreign seas and my home
is nowhere
I am a stranger to others, a stranger to myself, in this body I carry
I'm a hazard to my health
Who am I, for what purpose was I created, always left feeling
completely isolated?
I questioned this curse, why my mother gave birth to me, a mix
raced child
A breed banded so wild I grew up confused, my heart bruised
I've seen myself as just a child, blessed with sight,
And a vision to see beyond imperfections and beauty, I see me as
just me
Not defined by the colour of my skin or my ethnicity
I didn't even understand such words, culture and religion didn't
mean much back then
But the colour of your skin did, and the abuse I once received
scarred this once young kid

I was already struggling with my identity, I was called the half-caste and the half-caste kid
The mixed breed, what really was the need to cast me aside with the weeds because I was different
It took some time but I finally started to understand that I would have to rise above all the negativity to reach the love
I had to overcome the hate and start rewriting my own fate
I knew I'd never be fully accepted by both my white and Indian family
I was the misfit, the piece that didn't connect properly
Until I took charge of what controlled me
Now I embrace my ethnicity, no longer ashamed of me
I'm not dual heritage, I am mixed race and I'm fine if others want to say that to my face
I stand for what I speak when I say being mixed raced is unique
It took me many years to find comfort in my own skin and realise we are all beautiful for within
Being different is a damn good thing.

Let's Be The Change

Language connects us all, it starts with human communication
Deep conversations, connecting organisations
It starts with words, words and expression
And how first time impressions are so important
How listening is the key
To changing the past and re-creating a new mental health legacy
It starts with empathy, the first source of connection
Of building relationships and new directions
Making a difference, not just a new system
It's time to listen and find solutions
A new evolution, planting the seeds of new beginnings
Being that first point of contact
When people are drowning not swimming
Trying to reach the shore
Not falling, nor sinking or feeling ignored
Mental health is an illness,
An invisible sickness of the mind, body and soul
When you as a person are not fully in control of how you feel
And any cry for help is a cry to heal
It's these long waiting lists, waiting times to be assessed
That delayed appointment leads to crisis
It's about branching all the roots and linking networks together
So the trees you create can withstand any change in the weather
Seasons change just like our mental well being
And mental health is not all-seeing
Recovery takes time when trying to heal the mind
It starts with simplifying points of contact
And making services easier to find
It starts with people seen as people
Human interaction not clinical

Seeing as visible, being recognised as priority
Looked beyond an image, visually
Being heard, it starts with practitioners keeping their word
Not repeating the same old patterns
Let's not let that happen
And in this room is where it starts
Using your knowledge and experience but thinking
With your hearts
Today is where change starts.

Self-reflection Is A Bitch

When you have had a long-arsed day and it's your time to unwind
And leave of the day's stress behind, let the poison leave your DNA
Now your body tells you it's okay to sit back and destress
Leave the file of memories of the good and the bad in a shabby mess
There is no one to impress, it's just you and time
And you're desperately trying to unwind but then these thoughts start to kick in
Your mind is over analysing every bloody thing and you start over-thinking
Of what could have been, re visiting the same questions that you just didn't see
At that time you to start re-evaluate every word spoken
Hate that you can't change the conversation, the segments that were broken
But once again it's just me, questioning their thoughts in my mind
Things that probably weren't meant to be
Self-reflection is a bitch, that side digging stitch
I wish I could switch it off, just stop the thoughts in my head from multiplying
Always amplifying every damn conversation, the happy smiles, the intentional lies
That I can always see so visually because I can see the truth behind the eyes
Or can I? Is it that I pull apart every living memory till it makes sense to me
Over thinking till I'm drowning and I'm sinking, planting seeds in my own mind?
As my body's trying to unwind, trying to remind me I'm human too
You hear this little voice calling, this lioness roaring, telling you
You have to stop, stop thinking of what others think of you

Because what is the point in knowing what others do?
But self-reflection is a bitch, it's either that or I care too much
Or I hate the person that has got me over-questioning myself
in the first place
Invading my head space, it's time to release this wave
Of negative energy, for I am somebody if only to me
But that doesn't stop me thinking that
Self-reflection is a bitch.

The Earth Has No Borders

Its sweet lands and salty water
And we are planted like seeds on this earth
Yet some are more blessed than others at birth
Born in a time of corruption and lies
Hear the open cries of mankind, and the world stands silent
Lies have become the new truth
Rarely covered by the news unless it's a deported rescue
Division created on this sacred land, it's come to the point
We are told where we can and can't stand
Like we are not even born from this land
Well I take a stand and say, this land is for all
We should be free to live in any country where we feel safe
That's a healthy place for one to prosper and grow
Migrants don't want to be seen as another number or sentence on
your manifesto
They want to be heard and seen just like you, as another human being
It's where racism and division is created
When people feel segregated, yet one word as simple, as *hello*
Can build on relationships and help diversity grow
It can create links of life, and be the change of a new tomorrow
Where one can finally live in peace, welcoming refugees
Because all lives matter, no life carries any more value than another
We are all born innocent, free in the womb of our mothers
We are not born to hate and I'm telling you, no one wants to migrate
from their motherland
But in life we are not all dealt the same hand and the only safe option
is to leave, leave to safety
Leave so they can breathe a new day of hope, of security
Our differences do not divide us, they enrich our lives like art
enriches the soul

Society needs to realise that sometimes in life things happen
that are beyond our control
This world needs to bond like land meets sea
Where hate cannot discriminate and people are allowed
to live free.

Tired (PMT)

You're running on the last drop of energy, your body's feeling heavy
It's only 10am and you're wishing for this not to happen again
It's your biological clock and this month it's actually stopped on its due date
When you're feeling overweight and your emotions have physically exhausted your mental state
Your body's suffering from this constant backache
You know there is going to come a day when your hormones start to drop
And your body starts to build this rage and wish you could make it stop
Your emotions are spiralling in this destructive storm
The body's got this hot and cold thing going on and you just feel too warm
You have this high intense build up, these frequent emotional waves
That keep playing games with how you behave, one minute you're happy as can be
The next you're aggravated by everything that you see
To the point it affects you mentally
Then you have moments where you need to cry, you need to release
To feel any kind of inner peace, you have to let it go
Let the negative energy flow, allow it to leave
So you can just breathe at the very time you feel like your falling apart
When the very beat of your heart screams out
And you're consumed with this overactive thinking and self-doubt
You question why you're grabbing your third chocolate bar and it's only been
Ten minutes since u last stuffed your face and you're high on caffeine

Everything just seems to find a way to your mouth, no let me
rephrase that
Consuming all those unhealthy fats, not unable to look at
All those sweet sugars that find a way to your lips
Like sun meets moon that feeling is like total eclipse on a winter's
evening
PMT gets me feeling like I lose myself for Two weeks out of four
And it's something I cannot ignore, so I try to love myself a little
bit more
Show myself, patience, kindness and a little self-love.

Indestructible

I am a fortress, built from fire, driven from the depths of hell
I am the scattered ashes that have risen and released a wave
of thunder in every blood cell
I am the raging storm that sends the waves crashing hard against
the rocks
I am the taste you crave, that lingers on your lips, your forbidden
detox
Your forbidden fruit, your intoxicating poison that breathes death
into light
I am a soul quenching drink that seeks your appetite
I am indestructible, I have held my own breath under water till my
lungs could take no more
I have slayed every demon on the battlefield and I brought peace
instead of war
I'm the elements of life, the roots that are linked to the earth's core
I am the lightning bolt that crackles before
The thunders roars and the open sky pours its heavenly scent
I am more, I am indestructible and this soul is untouchable
This heart is living proof of every scar, every shard that has pierced
my skin
That has tried to penetrate this life within
I am indestructible, you mistake this fragile soul
It's shatterproof and in control of my own destiny
For I am the wild flames that cannot be tamed by today's society
I am immortal from the pain I've had to endure
Numb to my surroundings and so much more
I create new chapters like dead leaves that fall seasonally
I am the current that swirls and twists in the sea
And I made a promise to myself that I'd never allow anyone again to
fuck with me
Because I am indestructible.

Brand
new
poems

Nothing Lasts

So I'm appreciating right now
Not focusing on when or how
Life will resume
I'm just limiting the time i consume
On the daily news feeds
Not that i ever believe what i read
That fear wants to change my DNA
Block my lungs with mucus
Suppress my airway
I'm trying to live life my way
I go to sleep in the early hours of the morning
Awaiting a new day dawning
Even though the passing of yesterday
Was just a few aways away
I'm alive and I'm breathing
And still believing that better days
Will arrive
In its silence i thrive
Hibernation has always been good for me
But it kind of reminds me
Of the caged me
The person i fought to be free
Of, it gets me craving noise
Something to disperse my tranquility
It gets me yearning to live
Beyond these walls of brick and stone
Explore beyond the horizon
Sail into the unknown
I want to stand amongst the clouds and fill my soul
With each breath, i want to release
What i let control

(ME)
I want to release my anxiety
And dance in the rain
As the droplets drench my body
I set free that pain
Because right now everything
Has changed
I'm rewriting my own fate
Changing dates
And erasing everything
Without meaning
Using this time for healing
For building relationships
With myself
Not letting this lockdown mess
With my health
We are still living on
Borrowed time
Finally taking control
Of what i can
With this life of mine
Embracing the slow pace of time
Appreciating now
Because nothing lasts forever.

Do You Remember Me?

As night falls into darkness and stars light up the sky
Do you remember me when you walk in from work?
Closing the door shut
As you whisper the world goodbye
Do you, do you miss me when you see the rain falling
As it splashes on pavements, making swirling sensations?
As it bounces like airwaves
Do you miss me when you see her?
Do your emotions begin to stir
When she illuminates your eyes
In the sky?
Do you feel them, those feelings, as they intensify?
Does your soul scream out in despair
With your ego in doubt and your heart in need of repair?
Do you see me in the faces of leaves that fall in autumn?
Does it spark memories that you thought you had forgotten?
Do you remember me as winter turns colder
Like icicles sitting on your shoulders?
But you, always loved the seasons that were colder
Do miss me when you bathe
When the water splashes likes waves
Craving only its deserted island
Yet you stay silent
No breaking through
That cold ice cube
That cages you
Into wanting me.

September

The day my mother was born
And i mourn her life
Like winter mourns spring
Wishing i could bring
Her life new meaning
September rain falls
Like stones that plummet off
Mountain walls
As leaves that fall
Leaving naked branches
Curled into feathered twigs
Trees that are caged like
The human ribs
That sit grounded
September gives me this
Undescrible feeling
As summer's leaving
Most people start grieving
For the long summer evenings
Yet i, i awaken in the season
Of the chilly, cold, crisp air that paints
The sky with my breath
The air's never felt so fresh
As it does in September
It's like a new phase has started
To shake off what's departed
What serves no purpose
Like dead leaves scattered on the surface
That now seem worthless
As they crumble into dust
It somehow seems unjust

To see how their beauty can wither
Yet September never fails to deliver
To show us how beautiful this
Season can be
Even with naked, bare trees
And flowers that deplete into
Dried up roots leaving
Golden shrivelled twigs
That snap likes sticks
Where delicate flowers
Once blossomed
Now Autumn helps us to remember
The days may grow short in
September
Yet the sun will still shine its rays of light
between the long winter nights
We can still make this
An autumn to remember.

The Only Place I Want To Be

The only place I want to be
Is a place where
No lessons are taught
Pleasure over structure
Peace over disturbance
Release over restraint
The company of one over crowds
The only skills I want to be taught
Are the ones that excite my thoughts
The only text books I want to analyse
Are the ones that fertilise my soul
Beyond any physical control
The only place my ink wants to stain
Is every link and chain to your heart
The only lesson I want to learn
Is where Venus meets Mars?
Where love confuses science
And hearts are linked to stars?
The only path I want to walk upon
Is one that leads me to you
Where I rescue you
And you resuscitate me
Where your tongue speaks
In a language that connects to my body receptors
Igniting that deep ancestor's solar flare
A rebirth of galaxies created
In this universe we sparked
The only place I want to be
Is one where you are here
right next to me.

Broken

Let me stand with the lost, the broken
The peoples whose issues are unspoken
Let me raise my vocal chords in their silence
Send waves screeching like sirens
I stand with those hidden rocks
disguised as diamonds
A little rough around the edges
Ground deeply from the earth
The ones who don't realise
What their own life is worth
I'd rather stand with the broken
The needy
The ones who silently scream
Hear me
I'd rather walk with the lost
The ones who have suffered misfortune at such a cost
Yet still get back up like a tomorrow's sunrise
Like tonight's full moon,
Those who value life and have not been fed
From a silver-dipped spoon
I'd rather drink from the open sky
Listening to the hardship of those who cry
Who struggle to make ends meet but eventually get by
The ones who don't bullshit
To fit in with society's norms
The only generation left of the human form
People that are in need of a helping hand
Yet are given a life beating heart
One that's dissected into little pieces
Which releases more love that can ever be found
I'd rather surround myself with the broken.

It's More Than Nature For Me

It's not just nature
It's more than green leaves weaved
Into branches
It's more than protruding vines
That climb along the bark of the trees
It's more than what the eye can see
More than whispers of grass
That brush passed your skin
Leaving its delicate flicker
In your memory, its touch
That prickles as much
Leaving its imprint
Tattooed in your mind
It's more than nature
That I find draws me closer
Draws me into this
Whirlwind of peace
I drown in its heavenly
Scent, in its sweet silence
Where my mind
Is exercised by nature's guidance
It's more than just being outdoors
Where the mind explores
A universe on earth
With a sky that swirls into a canvas
Of blue and grey
Leaving a ray of summer's silk
Breaking through the clouds
It's my place away from the crowds
It's more than nature
It stimulates my behaviour

It releases something inside me
That connects me more than
The soil is connected to the trees
It's more than nature for me.

THANKYOUS

To my present self "SHE", I thank you, you survived this, with your heart intact and your soul full of passion and empathy for others. You made it through your fear and I'm so proud of you

Thank you to Stuart at The Verve Poetry Press for seeing something in me and for making SHE possible.

I thank the Universe, the Earth my Creator, for my life, for every sunrise and every sunset that my eyes get to see. For every crashing wave I get to bathe in. For every season that passes and every year I am blessed to reach.

To my family my strength is in your love, thank you for support and encouragement always, im here because you believed in me.

I thank every single person I have come across in my life, your kindness helped me grow and your No's taught me to keep fighting for what I believe in.

Thank you to all my friends and everyone who has supported me along this journey,. People don't always realise the impact of what they say or do and I would just like to say a huge thank you to you all. I appreciate your support and encouragement over the years even when I doubted myself. Thank you

To my dear poetry friend Peter Haney you are deeply missed

ABOUT VERVE POETRY PRESS

Verve Poetry Press is a quite new and already award-winning press that focussed initially on meeting a local need in Birmingham - a need for the vibrant poetry scene here in Brum to find a way to present itself to the poetry world via publication. Co-founded by Stuart Bartholomew and Amerah Saleh, it now publishes poets from all corners of the UK - poets that speak to the city's varied and energetic qualities and will contribute to its many poetic stories.

Added to this is a colourful pamphlet series, many featuring poets who have performed at our sister festival - and a poetry show series which captures the magic of longer poetry performance pieces by festival alumni such as Polarbear, Matt Abbott and Geraldine Carver.

In 2019 the press was voted Most Innovative Publisher at the Saboteur Awards, and won the Publisher's Award for Poetry Pamphlets at the Michael Marks Awards.

Like the festival, we strive to think about poetry in inclusive ways and embrace the multiplicity of approaches towards this glorious art.

www.vervepoetrypress.com
@VervePoetryPres
mail@vervepoetrypress.com